# FARTING MAGICAL CREATURES

**Magical creatures have farts too.
This is just a fact.**

Copyright © 2017 by Eclectic Esquire Media, LLC
www.MTLottBooks.com

ISBN: 978-1-951728-07-6

No part of this publication may be reproduced, distributed or transmitted in any form or by any means, without the prior written permission of the publisher, except in the case of brief quotations embodied in critical reviews and certain other noncommerical uses permitted by copyright law.

## Share your colored pages on instagram @mtlottbooks

## Sign up for free coloring pages at www.MTLottBooks.com

## Connect with M.T. Lott on facebook
www.facebook.com/authormtlott

# BOOKS BY M.T. LOTT

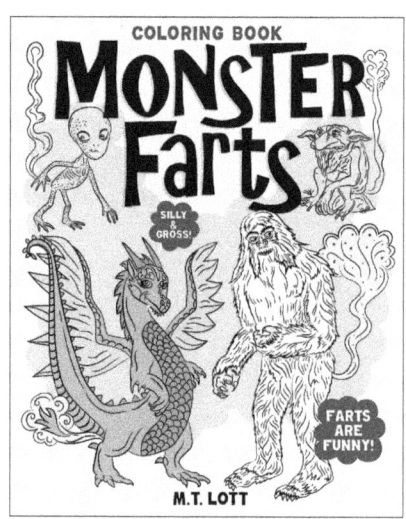

**Available for purchase at your favorite on-line bookstore.**

FACT: Brownies have terrible gas — but they like it.

FACT: Sometimes when a dragon farts, a little fire comes out.

FACT: Hippogriffs use their wings to blow the smell away.

FACT: Troll farts are tremendous.

FACT: Boy centaurs are gross.

**FACT: Technically, a Basilisk farts out of its scent glands.**

FACT: Griffin farts are quite medieval.

FACT: The seals prefer when Selkies pass gas out of the ocean.

FACT: A phoenix has a very fiery blast.

FACT: Sea foam is Hippocamp gas.